CARS, CARS, CARS

FAST CARS

by Barbara Alpert

Gail Saunders-Smith, PhD, Consulting Editor

Consultant: Leslie Mark Kendall, Curator
Petersen Automotive Museum
Los Angeles, California

CAPSTONE PRESS
a capstone imprint

Pebble Plus is published by Capstone Press,
1710 Roe Crest Drive, North Mankato, Minnesota 56003.
www.capstonepub.com

Library of Congress Cataloging-in-Publication Data
Alpert, Barbara.
 Fast cars / by Barbara Alpert.
   p. cm.—(Pebble plus. Cars, cars, cars)
 Summary: "Simple text and color photographs describe nine fast cars"—Provided by the publisher.
 Audience: Grades K-3.
 Includes bibliographical references and index.
 ISBN 978-1-62065-086-8 (library binding)
 ISBN 978-1-62065-873-4 (paperback)
 ISBN 978-1-4765-1074-3 (eBook PDF)
 1. Sports cars—Juvenile literature. I. Title. II. Series: Pebble plus. Cars, cars, cars.
 TL236.A47 2013
 629.222—dc23   2012032227

Editorial Credits
Erika L. Shores, editor; Kyle Grenz, designer; Laura Manthe, production specialist

Photo Credits
Alamy: culture-images GmbH, 9; Corbis: Transtock, 13; Dreamstime: Mmc12, 5, 19; Newscom: ZUMA Press/Toronto Star/Rene Johnston, 7; Photo Courtesy of Hennessey Performance, 17; Shutterstock: Gustavo Fadel, cover (left), Max Earey, 21, oksana.perkins, cover (right); Wikimedia: Nate Hawbaker, 15, richard, 11

Artistic Effects
Shutterstock: 1xpert

Editor's Note: Top speeds listed are recorded as of 2012.

Note to Parents and Teachers

The Cars, Cars, Cars set supports national science standards related to science, technology, and society. This book describes and illustrates fast cars. The images support early readers in understanding the text. The repetition of words and phrases helps early readers learn new words. This book also introduces early readers to subject-specific vocabulary words, which are defined in the Glossary section. Early readers may need assistance to read some words and to use the Table of Contents, Glossary, Read More, Internet Sites, and Index sections of the book.

Printed in the United States of America in North Mankato, Minnesota.
072018   000757

Table of Contents

Fast

Zip! Zoom! Squeal! Vroom!
What are the fastest cars
on the road?

A Lamborghini Aventador reaches
62 miles (100 kilometers) per hour
in 3 seconds. That's three times
faster than most cars.

**Say it like this: Lamborghini Aventador
(lam-bor-GHEE-nee a-VEN-ta-dor)**

Top speed: 217 miles (349 kilometers) per hour

A Ferrari Enzo's doors open up
like giant butterfly wings.
The car looks as if it could fly
down the road.

Say it like this: Ferrari Enzo (fer-RA-ri EN-zoh)

Top speed: 217 miles (349 kilometers) per hour

Could a car drive upside down in a tunnel? The makers of the Gumpert Apollo say this fast car is built to do it.

Top speed: 224 miles (360 kilometers) per hour

Faster

A Noble M600 is lightweight
and super fast. It reaches
120 miles (193 kilometers)
per hour in under 9 seconds.

Top speed: 225 miles (362 kilometers) per hour

The engine bay of a McLaren F1

is lined with real gold foil.

The foil keeps the engine

from getting too hot.

Top speed: 242 miles (389 kilometers) per hour

The fastest car made
in the United States is
the SSC Ultimate Aero.
It was the world's fastest car
from 2007 to 2010.

Top speed: 257 miles (414 kilometers) per hour

Fastest

A Hennessey Venom GT weighs less than 2,800 pounds (1,270 kilograms). At top speed, drivers feel like they're being fired from a cannon.

Top speed: 260 miles (418 kilometers) per hour

A Koenigsegg Agera R is

a mighty machine.

The car's wheels act like

fans to cool the brakes.

Say it like this: Koenigsegg Agera (KOH-nig-segg A-gear-a)

Top speed: 260 miles (418 kilometers) per hour

Don't blink! You might miss

the Bugatti Veyron Super Sport

as it zooms by you. At top speed,

it uses more than 1 gallon

(3.8 liters) of gas every minute.

Say it like this: Bugatti Veyron (boo-GAH-tee VAY-ron)

**Top speed: 267 miles
(430 kilometers) per hour**

Glossary

brake—a part that slows down or stops a vehicle

cannon—a large, heavy gun with a metal tube that fires from an aircraft or tank

engine—a machine that makes the power needed to move something

engine bay—the space inside a car where the engine is kept

foil—metal that has been made into a thin, bendable sheet

Read More

Doman, Mary Kate. *Cool Cars.* All about Big Machines. Berkeley Heights, N.J.: Enslow Elementary, 2012.

Savery, Annabel. *Supercars.* It's Amazing! Mankato, Minn.: Smart Apple Media, 2013.

Von Finn, Denny. *Super Cars.* The World's Fastest. Minneapolis: Bellwether Media, 2010.

Internet Sites

FactHound offers a safe, fun way to find Internet sites related to this book. All of the sites on FactHound have been researched by our staff.

Here's all you do:

Visit *www.facthound.com*

Type in this code: 9781620650868

Super-cool stuff! Check out projects, games and lots more at www.capstonekids.com

Index

Word Count: 213
Grade: 1
Early-Intervention Level: 24